MASTER YOUR EMOTION

A practical guide for mastering your emotions and achieving inner peace

Dr. Smart Joseph

The information contained in this book is based on the author's experiences and opinions, and is provided for educational and entertainment purposes only. The author and publisher make no representations or warranties of any kind, express or implied, with respect to the completeness, accuracy, or reliability of the contents of this book. The author and publisher will not be held liable for any damages resulting from the use of the information contained in this book.

This book is not intended as a substitute for professional advice, such as legal, financial, or medical advice. Always seek the assistance of qualified professionals when making important decisions or taking actions that may have significant consequences.

Table of Contents

Introduction

Imagine feeling overwhelmed, anxious, and stressed out on a daily basis. Every little thing seems to set you off, and you struggle to control your emotions. You feel disconnected from yourself and those around you.

But what if there was a way to change all of that? What if you could learn to master your emotions and achieve inner peace?

In "Master Your Emotion: Strategies for Mastering Your Emotions and Achieving Inner Peace," you will discover practical techniques and strategies for taming your emotions and finding balance in your life. Through mindfulness, self-reflection, support, self-care, and healthy coping mechanisms, you can learn to better understand and manage your emotions, leading to a happier, more fulfilling life.

This book is not just a theoretical guide, but a practical toolkit filled with actionable steps that you can start implementing today. So if you're ready to take control of your emotions and achieve inner peace, this book is for you. The journey towards mastering your emotions may not be easy, but it is certainly worth it.

The importance of mastering your emotions

Mastering your emotions is important for a number of reasons. It can help you maintain better relationships with others, make more informed decisions, and lead a more fulfilling life. When you are able to control your emotions, you are better able to communicate effectively and handle difficult situations with grace. Additionally, mastering your emotions can help reduce stress and improve your overall mental health and well-being.

The benefits of inner peace

Inner peace refers to a state of being free from turmoil or disturbance. When you have inner peace, you feel calm, centered, and at ease with yourself and the world around you. There are numerous benefits to achieving inner peace, including:

- ❖ Improved mental health: Inner peace can help reduce stress, anxiety, and negative emotions, leading to better mental health and overall well-being.

- ❖ Greater clarity and focus: Inner peace allows you to clear your mind and focus on the present moment, leading to increased productivity and better decision-making skills.
- ❖ Enhanced relationships: Inner peace can help improve your relationships with others, as you are better able to communicate and connect with others in a positive way.
- ❖ Increased happiness: Inner peace leads to a greater sense of contentment and happiness as you are able to let go of negative thoughts and emotions.

Overall, inner peace allows you to live a more fulfilling and joyful life.

Chapter 1: Mindfulness

Mindfulness is the practice of bringing one's attention to the present moment in a non-judgmental way. It involves paying attention to one's thoughts, feelings, and surroundings in a curious and accepting manner. The goal of mindfulness is to increase self-awareness and cultivate a sense of calm and clarity. Mindfulness can be practiced through various techniques, such as meditation, deep breathing, and mindful movement. Research has shown that mindfulness can have numerous benefits, including reducing stress, improving mental health, and increasing well-being.

The science behind mindfulness

Mindfulness has gained increasing attention in recent years, and a growing body of research has begun to explore the benefits of mindfulness and the underlying mechanisms behind these effects.

One of the main ways that mindfulness is thought to benefit mental health is through its ability to regulate emotions. When we experience negative emotions, such as stress or anxiety, it can be easy to get caught up in a cycle of negative thoughts and behaviors. Mindfulness can help disrupt this cycle by increasing awareness of one's thoughts and emotions and teaching individuals to respond to these emotions in a more balanced and accepting way.

Additionally, mindfulness has been found to activate the prefrontal cortex, a region of the brain involved in decision-making, problem-solving, and regulating emotions. This activation can lead to increased focus and attention, as well as a greater sense of control over one's thoughts and actions.

Overall, the science suggests that mindfulness can be a powerful tool for improving mental health and well-being.

How to practice mindfulness

There are many ways to practice mindfulness, and it can be helpful to find a method that works best for you. Here are a few ideas to get you started:

1. Meditation: This can be as simple as finding a quiet place to sit and focusing on your breath for a few minutes. You can also try guided meditations or apps like Headspace or Calm.

2. Deep breathing: Take a few deep breaths, focusing on the sensation of the air moving in and out of your body. You can do this anywhere, at any time.
3. Mindful movement: Engage in activities like yoga or tai chi, which incorporate mindfulness into the physical movements.
4. Pay attention to your senses: Take a few minutes to focus on what you see, hear, smell, taste, and touch. This can help bring your attention to the present moment.

Remember, the goal of mindfulness is not to eliminate thoughts or emotions but rather to increase awareness of them and respond to them in a non-judgmental way. Practice regularly, and be patient with yourself as you develop this skill.

Chapter 2: Self-reflection

Self-reflection is the practice of examining one's thoughts, feelings, and behaviors in order to gain insight and understanding. It can be a powerful tool for personal growth and development, as it allows individuals to gain a deeper understanding of themselves and how they relate to the world around them.

Self-reflection can help individuals identify patterns in their thoughts and behaviors, both positive and negative. By becoming aware of these patterns, individuals can make conscious choices about how to change or reinforce them. For example, if an individual realizes that they often get anxious before giving presentations, they can reflect on the underlying beliefs and behaviors that contribute to this anxiety and work to change them.

In addition to helping individuals identify patterns, self-reflection can also help increase self-awareness, empathy, and emotional intelligence. It allows individuals to better understand their own emotions and how they affect their actions and interactions with others.

Overall, self-reflection is a valuable skill that can lead to personal growth and increased well-being.

Identifying your emotional patterns

Identifying your emotional patterns involves examining your thoughts, feelings, and behaviors over time in order to recognize recurrent themes. This can be helpful in understanding the underlying causes of your emotions and the situations that tend to trigger them.

To identify your emotional patterns, try keeping a journal or record of your emotions on a daily basis. This can be as simple as jotting down a few notes about your emotional state at the end of each day. As you do this over time, look for patterns or themes that emerge. For example, do you tend to feel anxious before important deadlines or social events? Do certain people or situations consistently trigger negative emotions for you?

It can also be helpful to talk to someone you trust, such as a friend, family member, or therapist, about your emotional patterns. They may be able to provide insight and perspective that you haven't considered.

Once you have identified your emotional patterns, you can begin to explore the underlying beliefs and behaviors that contribute to them. This can help you make conscious choices about how to change or reinforce these patterns in order to improve your emotional well-being.

Changing unhealthy beliefs and behaviors

Changing unhealthy beliefs and behaviors can be challenging, but it is an important step in improving emotional well-being. Here are a few strategies that may be helpful:

- Set specific and achievable goals: Identify specific behaviors or beliefs that you would like to change and set specific, achievable goals for making these changes. For example, instead of resolving to "be less anxious," set a goal to "take 5 deep breaths and practice a relaxation technique for 5 minutes each day."
- Self-compassion: Be gentle and understanding with yourself as you work to change negative beliefs and behaviors. Remember that change is a process and that it is normal to make mistakes along the way.

- Seek support: Working with a therapist or joining a support group can be helpful in making changes to unhealthy beliefs and behaviors. These individuals can provide guidance and accountability as you work towards your goals.
- Replace negative thoughts with positive ones: When negative thoughts arise, try to reframe them in a more positive way. For example, instead of telling yourself, "I can't do this," try saying, "I may not be able to do this perfectly, but I can try my best and learn from any mistakes."

Remember, changing unhealthy beliefs and behaviors takes time and effort, but it is worth it for the benefits it can bring to your emotional well-being.

Chapter 3: Seeking Support

Seeking support refers to actively seeking out and engaging with individuals or resources that can provide emotional support and guidance. This can be an important step in managing your emotions and improving your well-being.

There are many ways to seek support, including:

1. Talking to friends and family: Sharing your feelings with trusted loved ones can provide a sense of connection and validation.
2. Joining a support group: Support groups, such as those for individuals with mental health challenges or for people going through a similar experience, can provide a sense of community and a safe space to share your feelings.
3. Working with a therapist: A trained professional can provide a safe, confidential space to discuss your emotions and help you develop coping strategies.
4. Seeking online resources: There are many online resources, such as forums, blogs, and helplines, that can provide support and guidance.

Remember, seeking support is a sign of strength and an important step in managing your emotions and improving your well-being. Don't be afraid to reach out and ask for help when you need it.

The importance of a support network

A support network refers to the people in your life who offer love, support, and guidance. Having a strong support network can be beneficial in many ways, including:

- ❖ Providing emotional support: Your support network can be there for you when you are feeling down or overwhelmed, offering a listening ear and a shoulder to lean on.
- ❖ Offering guidance and perspective: Your support network can help you see things from a different perspective, offering advice and guidance when you need it.
- ❖ Encouraging personal growth: Your support network can encourage and support you in your personal and professional goals, helping you grow and develop as an individual.

- ❖ Reducing stress: Having a supportive network of people can help reduce stress and improve mental health.

Overall, having a support network is an important aspect of emotional well-being. It can provide a sense of connection, validation, and belonging that is essential for healthy emotional functioning.

Finding and building a support system

Finding and building a support system involves actively seeking out individuals and resources that can provide emotional support and guidance. This may include friends and family, support groups, therapists, and online resources.

To build a strong support system, it can be helpful to:

- ❖ Identify your needs: Consider what type of support you are looking for and what you hope to gain from your support system.
- ❖ Be open and honest: Share your feelings and needs with those in your support system, and be open to their support and guidance.

- ❖ Be willing to offer support: Building a support system is a two-way street. Be willing to offer support to others in your network, as this can strengthen your relationships and create a sense of community.
- ❖ Seek out new connections: Don't be afraid to reach out to new people or resources that may be able to provide support. This can be especially important if your current support system is limited.

Remember, building a support system takes time and effort, but it is an important aspect of emotional well-being.

Sharing your emotions with others

Sharing your emotions with others refers to the act of expressing your feelings to someone you trust, such as a friend, family member, or therapist. This can be an important step in managing your emotions and improving your well-being.

There are many benefits to sharing your emotions with others, including:

- ❖ Providing a sense of connection: Sharing your emotions with others can create a sense of connection and intimacy, leading to a stronger sense of belonging and support.
- ❖ Offering a different perspective: Sharing your emotions with others can provide a new perspective on your feelings and experiences, leading to a better understanding of yourself and your emotions.
- ❖ Reducing stress: Sharing your emotions with a supportive listener can help reduce stress and improve mental health.
- ❖ Promoting self-awareness: Sharing your emotions with others can help increase self-awareness, as it requires you to examine and express your feelings in a more conscious and deliberate way.

It is important to remember that not everyone may be comfortable with or able to support you in the way that you need. It is okay to seek out multiple sources of support and to set boundaries with those who are not able to offer the support that you need.

Chapter 4: Self-care

"Self-care" refers to the practice of taking care of your physical, emotional, and mental well-being. It is an important aspect of maintaining overall health and happiness and can include activities such as:

1. Exercise: Engaging in physical activity can improve physical and mental health and help reduce stress.
2. Eating well: A healthy diet can provide the nutrients your body needs to function at its best.
3. Getting enough sleep: Adequate sleep is essential for physical and mental health.
4. Engaging in hobbies and activities that bring joy: Taking time to pursue activities that you enjoy can help reduce stress and improve well-being.
5. Setting boundaries: It is important to set limits on the demands placed on your time and energy in order to prioritize self-care.

Self-care can look different for everyone, and it is important to find activities that work for you and that you enjoy. Remember, self-care is not selfish–it is necessary for maintaining physical, emotional, and mental well-being.

The link between self-care and emotional well-being

There is a strong link between self-care and emotional well-being. Engaging in self-care activities can help improve emotional health in a number of ways:

- Reducing stress: Self-care activities, such as exercise, meditation, and hobbies, can help reduce stress and improve mental health.
- Improving mood: Engaging in activities that bring joy and pleasure can improve mood and overall well-being.
- Increasing self-esteem: Taking care of yourself can help boost your self-esteem and confidence.
- Providing a sense of control: Engaging in self-care activities can help individuals feel more in control of their lives, which can improve emotional well-being.

Overall, self-care is an important aspect of maintaining emotional well-being. By taking care of your physical, emotional, and mental health, you can improve your overall sense of well-being and happiness.

Practicing self-care on a daily basis

Here are some additional suggestions for practicing self-care on a daily basis:

1. Make time for activities that you enjoy and that help you relax, such as reading, taking a bath, or going for a walk.
2. Set aside time each day to do something that nourishes your mind, body, and spirit, such as meditate, exercise, or spend time in nature.
3. Get enough sleep by creating a relaxing bedtime routine and setting a consistent sleep schedule.
4. Eat a healthy, balanced diet, and stay hydrated.
5. Take breaks from screens and technology to give your eyes and brain a rest.
6. Practice deep breathing or other relaxation techniques to reduce stress and improve your mood.

7. Seek support from friends, family, or a therapist when you need it.

Remember, self-care looks different for everyone, so it's important to find what works for you. The key is to make self-care a priority and to incorporate it into your daily routine.

Chapter 5: Coping Mechanisms

Coping mechanisms are the strategies that people use to manage and deal with stress, difficult emotions, and challenging situations. Some common coping mechanisms include:

- ❖ Exercise or engage in physical activity: This can help reduce stress and improve mood.
- ❖ Seek social support: Talking to friends, family, or a therapist can provide emotional support and help you feel less alone.
- ❖ Engage in relaxation techniques: This can include deep breathing, meditation, or yoga, which can help reduce stress and improve mental well-being.
- ❖ Practice self-care: Taking care of your physical and mental health can help you feel more resilient and better equipped to handle stress.
- ❖ Use positive self-talk: Reminding yourself of your strengths and abilities can help you feel more positive and confident.
- ❖ Set goals and prioritize tasks: Having a sense of purpose and structure can help you feel more in control and less overwhelmed.

- ❖ Find healthy ways to cope with emotions: This can include journaling, expressing emotions through art or music, or finding healthy outlets for emotions like anger or frustration.

Remember, it's important to find coping mechanisms that work for you and to use them regularly to manage stress and maintain mental well-being.

The role of coping mechanisms in managing emotions

Coping mechanisms can play a vital role in managing emotions. When we are faced with stress or difficult emotions, it can be tempting to turn to unhealthy behaviors such as substance abuse or emotional eating to cope. However, these behaviors can often make things worse in the long run.

On the other hand, healthy coping mechanisms can help us manage our emotions in a more constructive way. For example, engaging in relaxation techniques can help us calm our minds and bodies and better manage our emotions. Seeking social support can also help us feel less alone and provide a sense of connection and belonging.

By using healthy coping mechanisms, we can learn to identify and express our emotions in a healthy way and develop more effective strategies for managing stress and difficult emotions. This can lead to improved mental well-being and overall quality of life.

Healthy coping strategies

Here are some healthy coping strategies that can help you manage stress and emotions:

1. Exercise or engage in physical activity: This can help reduce stress and improve mood.
2. Seek social support: Talking to friends, family, or a therapist can provide emotional support and help you feel less alone.
3. Engage in relaxation techniques: This can include deep breathing, meditation, or yoga, which can help reduce stress and improve mental well-being.
4. Practice self-care: Taking care of your physical and mental health can help you feel more resilient and better equipped to handle stress.

5. Use positive self-talk: Reminding yourself of your strengths and abilities can help you feel more positive and confident.
6. Set goals and prioritize tasks: Having a sense of purpose and structure can help you feel more in control and less overwhelmed.
7. Find healthy ways to cope with emotions: This can include journaling, expressing emotions through art or music, or finding healthy outlets for emotions like anger or frustration.
8. Practice gratitude: Focusing on the things you are grateful for can help you feel more positive and resilient.

Remember, it's important to find coping strategies that work for you and to use them regularly to manage stress and maintain mental well-being.

When to seek professional help

There are a few signs that it may be time to seek professional help for stress, emotions, or mental health concerns:

- ❖ If your coping mechanisms are no longer effective: If you are struggling to manage your emotions and stress despite trying various coping strategies, it may be helpful to seek professional help.

- ❖ If you are experiencing persistent negative emotions: If you are struggling with persistent feelings of sadness, anxiety, or hopelessness, it may be a sign that you could benefit from professional help.
- ❖ If your daily functioning is impaired: If your stress or emotional struggles are interfering with your daily life, such as your ability to work, go to school, or maintain relationships, it may be time to seek help.
- ❖ If you are experiencing thoughts of self-harm or suicide: If you are having thoughts of harming yourself or ending your life, it is important to seek immediate help. This could include calling a crisis hotline or seeking help from a mental health professional.

If you are experiencing any of these signs, it is important to reach out for help. There are many resources available, such as therapy or support groups, that can provide the support you need. It is never too late to seek help, and there is no shame in seeking support to improve your mental well-being.

Conclusion

Here is a recap of key strategies for mastering your emotions:

1. Practice mindfulness: This involves being present in the moment and paying attention to your thoughts and feelings without judgment.
2. Use positive self-talk: Reminding yourself of your strengths and abilities can help you feel more positive and confident.
3. Engage in relaxation techniques: This can include deep breathing, meditation, or yoga, which can help reduce stress and improve mental well-being.
4. Practice self-care: Taking care of your physical and mental health can help you feel more resilient and better equipped to handle stress.
5. Seek social support: Talking to friends, family, or a therapist can provide emotional support and help you feel less alone.
6. Find healthy ways to cope with emotions: This can include journaling, expressing emotions through art or music, or finding

healthy outlets for emotions like anger or frustration.

7. Set goals and prioritize tasks: Having a sense of purpose and structure can help you feel more in control and less overwhelmed.
8. Practice gratitude: Focusing on the things you are grateful for can help you feel more positive and resilient.

Remember, it's important to find strategies that work for you and to use them regularly to manage your emotions and maintain mental well-being.

Also, achieving inner peace is a journey, and it may take time and effort to find what works for you. It is important to be patient with yourself and to seek support when needed.

Final thoughts and encouragement

I hope these suggestions have been helpful in your journey towards mastering your emotions and finding inner peace. Remember that everyone's path to emotional well-being is unique, and it may take time and effort to find what works for you. It is important to be patient with yourself and to seek support when needed.

Remember that it is okay to feel a full range of emotions, and it is important to allow yourself to feel and express your emotions in a healthy way. By practicing self-care and using healthy coping mechanisms, you can learn to manage your emotions and find greater peace and well-being.

I encourage you to keep working towards your goals and to be kind to yourself along the way. You are capable of achieving inner peace and emotional well-being, and it is never too late to start working towards it.

www.ingramcontent.com/pod-product-compliance
Lightning Source LLC
LaVergne TN
LVHW052114160826
845678LV00015B/3547

* 9 7 9 8 3 7 3 2 0 0 1 3 4 *